EXPEDITION TO THE PAWNEE PICT VILLAGE

IN 1834

This booklet is Wagner-Camp No. 51, listed under the author, Thompson B. Wheelock, 1834, with the title: *Journal of Colonel Dodge's Exposition from Fort Gibson to the Pawnee Pict Village.* It was first printed in the Report of the Secretary of War attached to the President's Message of December 2, 1834, where it occupies pages 73 to 93, of Senate Executive Document 1, Twenty-third Congress, Second Session, Serial 266. It was also printed in American State Papers, Military Affairs, Volume V, pages 373 to 382. This rare booklet is not listed in Wright Howes' *U.S.IANA 1650-1950,* but it is mentioned on page 318 under Kingsbury, Gaines P. A typescript of the booklet was furnished by Jim Dowd of St. Charles, Illinois.

Of this edition 390 copies were printed.

This is Copy Number____94____.

EXPEDITION TO THE PAWNEE PICT VILLAGE IN 1834

Thompson B. Wheelock

YE GALLEON PRESS

FAIRFIELD, WASHINGTON

1978

ISBN 0-87770-198-9

REPORT OF
THE SECRETARY OF WAR

(Document No. 2.)

Journal of Colonel Dodge's Expedition from Fort Gibson to the Pawnee
Pict village.

Fort Gibson, August 26, 1834.

To Colonel Henry Dodge, U.S. Dragoons:

COLONEL: In obedience to your instructions, I have made, and have the honor herewith to present to you, a journal of the campaign of the regiment of dragoons for the summer of 1834.

With great respect,
Your obedient servant,
T. B. WHEELOCK,
1st. Lieut. Dragoons.

In consequence of the late arrivals of the companies from Jefferson barracks, the regiment did not move as early as could have been wished.

The nine companies destined for the campaign, (Captain Wharton's company "A" marched in May to escort a body of traders to Santa Fe,) began their movement from Camp Jackson on the 15th of June,

June 15: and, under the direction of the field and company officers, encamped on the west bank of the Arkansas, three miles from Fort Gibson; thence moved eighteen miles westwardly, to Camp Rendezvous. Strength of the regiment about five hundred.

Arrangement of officers for the campaign.

Colonel—Henry Dodge.
Lt. Colonel—S. W. Kearney.
Major—R. B. Mason.
Staff. Adjutant—1st Lt. J. W. Hamilton.
Ordnance Officer, &c.—1st Lt. T. B. Wheelock.
Acting Ass't. Quartermaster—1st Lt. Thomas Swords.
Acting Ass't. Com. Subsistence—2d Lt. John S. Van Deveer.
Company Officers. Company "B"—Capt. Sumner, 2d Lt. Burgwin, Bt. 2d Lt. McClure.
Company "C"—Capt. Duncan, Br. 2d Lt. Bowman.
Company "D"—Capt. Hunter, 1st Lt. Moore, 2d Lt. Steen.
Company "E"—Capt. Perkins, Bt. 2d Lt. Kingsbury.
Company "F"—1st Lt. Davis, Bt. 2d Lt. Eastman, 2d Infantry.
Company "G"—1st Lt. Cooke, Bt. 2d. Lt. Territt.
Company "H"—Capt. Boone, Bt. 2d Lt. Ury.
Company "I"—Capt. Brown, Bt. 2d Lt. Edwards.
Company "K"—1st Lt. Izard, 2d Lt. Shaumburgh.

Eight companies (Company "K" was left at Camp Jackson to complete preparations for the march) were assembled at Camp Rendezvous on the evening of the 20th June.

June 21st.—Twenty-three men, pronounced by the surgeon unfit for the campaign, sent back to Fort Gibson. The regiment took up the line of march for the Washita, upon the new road made by Gen. Leavenworth, at 8 o'clock in the morning; moved 20 miles southwest; crossed the north fork of the Canadian; encamped one mile thence; difficulty with wagons ascending the bank of this stream; assistance of thirty or forty men required to each. Good water at our camp—great want of it on the road. Sounds of the rapids of the north fork cheering to men and horses. With the command seventy beeves. Face of the country to-day, in general, open rolling prairie, soil light; a few miles from our halt, much timber and stony land.

Agreeably to previous arrangements, four bands of Indians joined us to-day, viz. eleven Osages, eight Cherokees, six Delawares, and seven Senecas. These men are to serve as guides, hunters, and interpreters, also as representatives of their several nations, should we, as we hope to do, meet with the Pawnees; and thus open the way to a friendly understanding between these nations. Among these Indians are some of the elite of the nations to which they belong.

Dutch, chief of the Cherokee party, remarkable for personal beauty, daring character, and successful enterprises against the Osages.

George Bullett, or Pon-da-gne-se, is the principal man of the Delaware party.

Beatte, a Frenchman, who has lived nearly all his life among the Osages, has charge of this band, and is celebrated for his skill as a hunter.

De-nath-de-ago is the leader of the seven Senecas.

We take with us, under conduct of the Osages, two Indian girls. One a Kiowa, about fifteen years of age, captured by the Osages a year or two since; the other a Pawnee prisoner, about eighteen years of age, taken by the Osages five or six years ago.

The restoration of these captive girls to their respective nations will, it is expected, facilitate the intercourse aimed for, conciliate the Indians, and pave the way to desirable treaties.

Camp Cass. June 22nd.—The command marched at 9 o'clock, westwardly, fifteen miles. Capt. Brown's company ("I") left in rear on account of breaking down of company wagon—wagons great drawbacks to military expeditions. Route to-day chiefly through timber, here and there small prairies; water scarce; beds of creeks dry. Encamped at the foot of a prairie-mound, four hundred feet in height, from the summit of which is seen a magnificent valley, stretching in every direction some twenty-five or thirty miles: we found here good water and grazing.

June 23rd.—Marched from Camp Cass at 9 o'clock, west by south, 17 miles; alternate prairie and timber; water less scarce than before, but warm, of a milky color, and in pools.

June 24th.—The advance was sounded at 9 o'clock; marched 21 miles west by south, halted at 4 o'clock P.M. and encamped near good water and grazing—excellent spring, impregnated with sulphur and iron. Captain Brown's company joined us this morning; road to-day chiefly through timber; met two infantry soldiers going from the post at the mouth of the Little river to Fort Gibson.

June 25th.—Col. Dodge and staff reached Camp Canadian, on the west bank of the Canadian, 13 miles from last camp, at 12 o'clock; reported to Gen. Leavenworth, whom we found in camp; command came up at two o'clock. Road to-day through open, level prairie, well watered; crossed the Canadian half a mile below the mouth of Little river; Canadian two hundred yards wide, bed nearly dry, low banks; Indian name signifies "river without banks." Near the east side passed Lt. Holmes, 7th infantry, with a company of the 7th regiment of infantry. Lt. Holmes just commenced building a fort and quarters for two companies. At Camp Canadian another sulphur spring, and good grazing and water.

June 26th.—At half past 8 o'clock, Col. Dodge and part of his staff, and a detachment of about 20 dragoons and our bands of Indians, preceded the command, and found Gen. Leavenworth at Camp Osage, five miles south of Cave creek; halted at half past 5 o'clock P.M., thirty-two miles from Camp Canadian. Streams to-day frequent, and abundantly supplied. The regiment, under command of Lt. Col. Kearney, left camp at half past 8 o'clock; left twenty-seven sick men at Camp Canadian, with Assistant Surgeon Hailes and Lieut. Edwards in charge. Lieut. Cooke was left here sick. Ten miles from Camp Canadian passed a band of Osages, between 500 and 600 in number, employed in curing buffalo meat, second chief of the nation, "Black Dog," in command—famous as a warrior; two Osages joined us as volunteers.

June 27th.—Left Camp Osage (Gen. Leavenworth in company) at half past 6 o'clock; marched 23 miles westwardly, and encamped on a creek at the end of a thirteen mile prairie; limestone, excellent streams of water, and frequent; soil in general, since leaving Fort Gibson, light and sandy, but often rich, and well adapted to grain. Crossed Blue river 10 miles from Camp Osage; saw in the vicinity much rich iron ore scattered over the surface of the earth. Met with and killed the first buffalo seen since the commencement of the march. Mineralogy of the country, thus far, of secondary formation: sandstone, limestone, freestone, and slate.

June 28th.—Set out at 7 o'clock; marched westwardly 25 miles, encamped on Bois d'Arc creek; passed a herd of buffalo this morning, some thirty or forty in number—Indians with us killed six of them. Road to-day chiefly over brushy prairie and through timber, some open prairie, water plentiful and good; character of timber, in general, small—post oak and black jack, and some trees of Bois d'Arc, a wood valuable to Indians for bows—a yellow elastic wood, of great tenacity. Entered the Washita bottom eight miles on the day's route—elm trees, sycamores, and ash. Health of the party good.

CAMP WASHITA. Sunday, June 29th.—Marched fifteen miles west by south, reached Capt. Dean's camp (two companies of 3d infantry) a mile or two from the Washita, at half past 12 o'clock; encamped near him. Road to-day through timber and brushy prairie; limestone gave place to-day to red sandstone; saw more iron ore. Delightful spring near Capt. Dean's camp. Capt. Dean informs us that Pawnees have been seen in the neighborhood within a few days.

June 30th.—Gen. Leavenworth declares his intention of commanding in person the expedition to the Pawnee country. Learned that some companies of infantry were to accompany us. Lts. Northrop and Steen, with twenty dragoons, joined us from west side of Washita—report Pawnees seen in that direction. (Remained in camp.)

July 1st.—The regiment under Col. Kearney arrived at 10 o'clock. A. M. and encamped near the Washita. Our detachment joined main Camp Washita Forty-Five men and three officers sick—Lts. McClure, Eastman, and Ury. The surgeon attributes the sickness to exposure in the heat of the day. Seventy-five horses and mules disabled: rapid marching in the heat of the day, and poor grazing at night, are supposed to have been the causes. (Remained in camp.)

The "note of preparation" is now heard over the camp: All are engaged in making ready for a Pawnee chase.

July 2d.—Remained in camp.

July 3d.—Preparations for crossing the Washita: a platform upon two canoes fixed for that purpose. Whole day occupied with passage of the left wing; horse and mule lost in crossing. Capt. Trenor joined; Osborn, a deserter from "F" company, brought in by a party sent in pursuit of him; sutler's wagon arrived; Lts. Swords and Van Deveer arrived; great disappointment in not receiving by Lieut. Swords horse shoe nails—sent blacksmiths to fort Towson to make nails. Lieut. Edwards arrived with twenty-three men, who were left sick at the Canadian on the 26th ult.; men chiefly recovered; Lieut. Cooke had gone back to Fort Gibson on surgeon's certificate of ill health. (Remained in camp.)

July 4th.—The right wing of the regiment crossed the Washita. Command encamped about four miles west from Camp Washita. Four horses drowned; last wagon passed over after dark in the evening. The Washita is a narrow stream about forty-five yards in width; water of a dark red color, banks bold, shores miry—inconvenient landing for horses. Monsieur Beyrick, botanist, &c. joined us to-day, with the view of accompanying the regiment to the prairie. Mr. Catlin, portrait painter, is also with us.

Gen. Leavenworth declares his intention of sending Col. Dodge with two hundred and fifty men to the Pawnee villages. He changes his determination, to command in person. Left sick at Dean's camp, near the Washita, Lts. Swords, McClure, and Eastman. Left here men for duty, and sick.

July 5th.—Change of camp promises to improve the health of the command; fine range for our horses, who have suffered of late for want of good grazing. Our horses in general, though thin, are apparently well able, if treated with care, to perform the campaign before us; spirits of the officers and men good; sanguine expectations of a successful march upon the Pawnees. (Remained in camp.)

July 6th.—Moved westwardly eight miles, to Camp Leavenworth.

July 7th.—Marched at 4 o'clock P.M. westwardly five miles. Major Mason and a party of officers killed several buffalo. Gen. Leavenworth joined us a short time previous to setting out from Camp Leavenworth. Left him there. By his order the regiment was reorganized. Number of companies six, each consisting of forty-two rank and file. Left one hundred and nine men for duty, and eighty-six sick. Left the following named officers: Capt. Trenor in command, Lts. Shaumburgh (sick,) Ury (sick,) Bowman, Kingsbury, and Van Deveer.

Expedition to the Pawnee Pict Village

New arrangement of officers.

Field and staff, Col. Dodge, Lt. Col. Kearney, Maj. Mason, Lt. and Adj. Hamilton, and Lt. Wheelock, temporarily attached.

Company "B"—Capt. Sumner, Lt. Burgwin.

Company "C"—Capt. Duncan, Lt. Territt.

Company "D"—Capt. Hunter, Lts. Moore and Steen.

Company "E"—Capt. Perkins, Lt. Davis.

Company "H"—Capt. Boon, Lts. Izard and Northrop.

Company "I"—Capt. Browne, Lt. Edwards.

Company "G" and "K" were temporarily broken up, and divided amongst the six companies.

The command furnished with ten days' provisions and eighty rounds of cartridges per man; baggage reduced to lowest possible quantity; marched in two columns.

July 8th.—Waiting for lost horses. A stupid sentinel last night mistook a horse for a hostile Indian, fired at, and killed him; alarmed the camp, and sent off in a stampede the rest of the horses—recovered all, save ten. The men of the regiment are excellent material, but unused to the woods. They often discover deficiencies in this kind of service. Among the officers are several excellent woodsmen—talent of this kind is exceedingly valuable to the regiment. We found here chalk. (Remained in camp.)

July 9th.—The command marched at half past 8 o'clock, northwest course, fourteen miles. Col. Dodge this morning received instructions from Gen. Leavenworth to send back a field officer to command at Camp Leavenworth; Lt. Col. Kearney was ordered to report to Gen. Leavenworth for that duty. Ten men, whose horses were lost on the night of the 7th instant, were sent back to Camp Leavenworth.

Soon after starting this morning, several persons on horseback were discovered, supposed to be Pawnees; face of country, to-day, high and rolling prairie; encamped in a small prairie, in sight of a large mound, some three or four miles distant, bearing south 40 west.

July 10th.—Cross Timbers; course to-day west 16 miles; country rough and broken, with but little water; little rain last night and this morning; cloudy weather during the day; some buffalo killed during the day; not much water at camp.

C. B. Wheelock

July 11th.—Command divided into three columns; the right column under command of Major Mason, the centre column under Captain Hunter, the left column under command of Captain Sumner; country, to-day, small prairies, bushy ravines, scrubby oak ridges, want of good water on the road; bad water at camp to-night; several buffalo killed to-day; course to-day west, distance twenty miles.

July 12th.—Encamped in a grove of small open timber, near a fine grove; marched at 8 o'clock; course west, distance, twelve miles; slips of prairie, timber, and bushy thickets.

CAMP CHOCTAW. July 13th.—Passed though the last of the Cross Timbers, and entered upon the grand prairie; marched at half past 8 o'clock from Camp Choctaw, west by north twenty-three miles, and encamped on a creek; highly beautiful country, tolerably well watered; command impeded to-day by sick men in litters; Indians, supposed to be Pawnees, were seen to-day; wild horses in large herds; one of the Indian guides caught one of them; immense herds of buffalo; passed several springs of rock oil, (petroleum.) Command halted at 6 o'clock P. M.; rear guard did not come up until 10; kept back by the sick falling to the rear.

July 14th.—Marched at half past 8 o'clock, seventeen miles west; number of sick decreased; the command had advanced about half a mile, when, on a hill to our right, we discovered a party of horsemen; our spy-glasses soon determined them to be Indians; Colonel Dodge halted the columns, ordered a white flag, and with it he and his staff moved in the direction of the Indians; after some delay, one of the party advanced upon full gallop, bearing a white flag upon his lance; he proved to be a Spaniard, who early in life had been taken by the Camanches; Colonel Dodge received him kindly and through our interpreter, who spoke a little Spanish, made known to him our pacific disposition. Gradually the whole band, about thirty Indians, came to us and shook hands; they proved to be Camanches, discovered a good deal of alarm, and eagerness to convince us of their disposition to be friendly; they rode good horses, they were all armed with bows and arrows, and lances, and carried shields of buffalo hide. We inquired where their village was; they answered, "two days' journey," and seemed anxious to conduct us thither. In reply to our inquiries concerning the Pawnees, they seemed not

Expedition to the Pawnee Pict Village

to understand the term; told us the Toyash village was one day's journey from their camp; that they would send for the Toyash chiefs if we would accompany them to the camp. They signified, however, their desire to have Colonel Dodge wait with his command in their camp, and go on the next day. Colonel Dodge paid no regard to their requests, but showed an indifference to their movements, and an independence of them, which had the effect to make them follow us; they accompanied us. Found another band, making in all some forty or fifty; they told us that they were a very numerous people. Colonel Dodge told them that we were a very numerous people; that more troops were coming behind with large guns. After we halted to encamp for the night, they came to beg tobacco, and to talk with Colonel Dodge, who informed them "that the President, the great American captain, had sent him to shake hands with them; that he wished to establish peace between them and their red brethren around them, to send traders among them, and be forever friends." They shook hands with the Osages, Cherokees, Delawares, &c. who were with us, and seemed highly satisfied with their interview with us, and offered to accompany us to the Toyash village; country to-day beautiful, open prairie, game scarce, two or three deer were killed, no buffalo seen, a herd of wild horses passed near us; provision threatens to be scarce; Colonel Dodge anxious to expedite business lest his men may suffer on this account; one or two horses broke down to-day.

The Camanche is a fine looking Indian, in general naked; some of them wore blankets. The squaws are dressed in deer skins, and are good looking women, among them were several Spanish women; evidently long used to Camanche habits; appearance of a Camanche fully equipped on horseback, with his lance and quiver and shield by his side, is beautifully classic. This has been an interesting day to us, our goal seems in sight; uncertainty of reaching the Pawnees much lessened.

July 15th.—Marched at half past 7 o'clock, twenty-four miles northwest; severe rain last night; the Camanches left us this morning, with the exception of one who remained as guide; he assures us that we shall reach the Camanche camp to-morrow. Colonel Dodge learns that the Camanches, Kiowas, and the band called by us the Pawnee Picts, but correctly termed the Toyash, are friends, and to a certain degree allies, and mingle so as to be, except in language, much the same people; the Camanches are, we learn, the largest band, the proudest and boldest; therefore the Colonel has resolved to visit them first, thence to the Toyash village, establish friendly understandings with one or both, or war with one or both, as may be; officers and men on the alert, as if in the atmosphere of war.

July 16th. — Marched at 9 o'clock, halted at half past 2 o'clock, course north by west, distance twelve miles; an accident occurred in camp last night, Sergeant Cross was shot by a dragoon in the hip. We had marched three of four miles, when we discovered a party of Camanches on our left. Col. Dodge sent two officers to meet them and shake hands with them; they were a hunting party, some ten or twelve in number; they were brought to Col. Dodge; the columns were halted; they shook hands with the Colonel and his officers, and the Indians; we then moved on together for the Camanche camp; the Pawnee girl recognised an old acquaintance in the captain of this party, and rendered service by interpreting what he said, through the Osages. The Camanche captain informs us that it is but a short distance to their camp, his people wish to be our friends, &c.; two or three miles with our new friends brought us in sight of their camp, situated in a valley; here we met about a hundred mounted Camanches, who had come out to welcome us, and evidently not a little alarmed; we shook hands with them; the Cherokees, Osages, &c. advanced and performed the same ceremony, when we all moved together for their camp; on arriving at it, they invited us to cross the creek and encamp with them; Colonel Dodge, however, preferred leaving the creek between us and our red friends. This day has been a very interesting one, absolutely so, and peculiarly so, as we were anxious, impatient, and uncertain as to the movements of these Indians. Six nations, some of whom had but recently been at war with each other, shake hands together—a form, it is true, but a type, we believe, of a permanent peace that must promote the interest of all. Our camp "Camanche" an admirable position, the steep bank of a creek in front, and a ravine bounding the other three sides; habitual form of our camp a rectangle; horses picketed within it at night, and surrounded by a chain of sentinels; orders issued that no man should visit the Camanche camp, nor officer, without special permission. The Camanches have hoisted an American flag over their camp, which contains more than 200 skin lodges. Herds of horses, in all not less than 3,000, are grazing around them; they have been here evidently but a day or two; their chief is absent with a hunting party. We are now in sight of a chain of peaks, so called, mountains, bearing south and west; behind these are the Totash villages. Some of these hills cannot be less than 2,000 feet above the prairie at their base; number of sick, 29; in litters, 4. Our guide, yesterday, was not a little wavering in his disposition to serve us. Colonel Dodge presented him with a gun, which produced a fine effect upon his spirits; he could not hear the Pawnee girl; but no sooner was he in actual possession of the yauger, and felt the well filled cartridge box buckled around his body, than his grave face became wreathed with smiles, his sense of hearing was suddenly restored, his arms sawed the air with signs, and, through the magical influence of the gun, we gained several fragments of useful information. We are exceedingly unfortunate in not having an interpreter. Our Spanish interpreter, a Cherokee, is very imperfect.

July 17th.—Camanche chief still absent. Some of our officers purchased wild horses to-day. A blanket or butcher knife is equivelent to a horse. Waiting to-day for the Camanche chief to return to his camp. Col. Dodge hopes to be able to induce him to accompany us to the Toyash villages. The Kiowa girl is quite sick today. One of the Camanches informs us that their great chief will be here to-morrow when the sun is high, and that he can talk to the Kiowa and Pawnee girls. (Remained in camp.)

July 18th.—The chief has not arrived. Doubt somewhat the sincerity of the Spaniard, who informed us he would certainly come. The Camanches visit our camp, and trade with us. Monsieur Beyrick, the botanist, left us on the 7th inst. Number of sick today 33. Three officers sick. Waited for the chief until 11 o'clock, when the advance was sounded; marched 7 miles westwardly; found a Pawnee Mohaw, who has been to the Toyash village, and who promises to guide us thither.

Two miles from camp; command delayed two hours waiting for the litters to come up; six litters, including Mr. Catlin's. Remarkable absence, day and night, of musquitoes and flies. A chain of hills five miles from us, bearing south by west; country exceedingly beautiful; soil good;

water abundant; grazing excellent. The season is a remarkably dry one, but we have suffered very little for want of good water. Our men seem somewhat discontented on account of the scarcity of game; they are very improvident; brought ten days' provisions on the 7th, with orders to make it last 20 days; have been supplied with plenty of buffalo meat till within a day or two. Yet many of them are entirely out of provisions; plenty of deer in the neighborhood, but no buffalo; out of the buffalo range to-day; our sick encumbered us so much that Col. Dodge resolves to leave them behind.

July 19th.—Marched at 8 o'clock for the Toyash villages; command reduced to 183 men; left in sick camp, covered by a breastwork of felled timber, seventy-five men; thirty-nine of these sick; Lt. Moore left here sick; Surgeon Findlay for duty; Lt. Izard in command; left our jaded horses; marched 23 miles southwest; two miles from camp, began to ascend hills, apparently a ridge of mountains, running south by east; limestone; curious regularity of limestone upon the first hill passed over; rows of pavement resembling, at a little distance, furrows in a field; road rough, leading over rocky ravines, and close passes in the mountains; our guide seems to have chosen the most uneven and circuitous route; height of these mountains from 200 to 1,500 feet; wagons nor artillery could possibly pass these hills; halted at 3 o'clock, and encamped near a creek; a few miles before reaching our halting place for the night, the face of the country changed; secondary formation gave way entirely to primitive rock; mountains of granite, almost wholly without soil; upon the side of one of them, noticed a shining spot, apparently a waterfall, glistening in the sunlight; an old woodsman astonished us, by informing us it was a mass of salt; no buffalo; our unshod horses suffered very much to-day; wild horses in abundance, and bears; many deer were seen, a few were killed; scanty allowance of provisions for our men; we march too fast to be able to hunt much on the road; game is now divided among the command with great care; marched in three columns; baggage reduced to three pack horses to each company.

July 20th.—The command moved at half past 7 o'clock, west course; halted at half past 4 o'clock, 37 miles; road literally of granite rock for miles; after a few miles struck high prairies, thinly scattered with bushes;

then ravines and difficult passes; immense blocks of granite piled on each other, from 500 to 1,000 feet in height; many horses gave out to-day; traces of buffalo, but saw none; about the middle of the day's march the mountains became more detached; passed to-day what is called a "dog village." The prairie dog, or "marmot," is an animal somewhat larger than a squirrel, with a head like that of a dog; they live in holes in the ground, about 20 paces apart from each other; five or six miles were covered by the habitations of these little animals. We encamped five miles from the Toyash village, which is situated on a branch of Red river; soon after we had pitched our camp, Lt. Northrop was directed to pursue, and endeavor to bring to camp, an Indian who was discovered on horseback; Lt. Northrop, after some difficulty, induced the Indian, who proved to be of the Toyash nation, to accompany him; he was very much alarmed; conversed readily with the Pawnee girl. We behaved kindly to this Indian; assured of our friendly disposition, and allowed him to return to his village. The Toyash girl is now of very great service, as an interpreter. The band not coming out to meet us to-day, convinced us that they had either fled, or had determined to make a stand, and give us a fight; bayonets were fixed, and every preparation made for a conflict. Water to-day at our camp salt. Width of the branch of Red river about 500 feet from bank to bank; water low. Dutch, the Cherokee guide, very ill; the Kiowa girl ill also.

July 21st.—The command marched at 8 o'clock for the Toyash village; proceeded a mile or two, when we met about 60 Indians, who had come out to meet us; shook hands with them, and moved on in company with each other; they stated that the principal chief was absent on a visit to the Pawnee Mohaw's country; passed their cornfields on our way to their town; these fields are well cultivated, neatly enclosed, and very extensive, reaching, in some instances, several miles; we saw also here melons of different kinds, squashes &c. The Indians discovered a good deal of alarm as we approached their village; frequently halted, and begged Col. Dodge not to fire on them; Col. Dodge promised them safety. These Indians are chiefly naked, and are armed with bows and arrows. They have few horses, and seem altogether an unwarlike people. Before we started this morning, the uncle of the Pawnee girl rode up to our camp; he embraced his relation, and shed tears of joy on meeting her. We soon reached the village, which is situated immediately under mountains of granite, some 600 feet in height; in front of the village runs the river. We counted near 200 grass lodges; these are made of poles fixed firmly in the earth, fastened together at the top, and thatched substantially with prairie grass and stalks from their cornfields; many of these lodges are thirty feet high and forty feet in diameter; in the centre of the floor a shallow excavation serves as a fireplace; around the sides are comfortable berths, large enough to accomodate two persons each. We encamped on a fine position, about one mile from the village. Toyash men are less fine looking than the Camanches. Their women are prettier than the Camanche squaws; indeed, some of their girls are very pretty; naked, save a broad garment of dressed deer skin, or red cloth, worn about the middle; some of the men wear coats of red cloth, obtained from the Spaniards of Mexico. Most of our officers visited them on the day of our arrival, and were hospitably entertained. Our own provisions were almost entirely exhausted; we had met with little or no game for several days, and found most excellent fare in the dishes of corn and beans which they dress with buffalo fat; they served us thus liberally, and for dessert gave us watermelons and wild plums. Our men purchased green corn, dried horse meat and buffalo meat; we depended, during our stay with them, on their dried meat and corn, which, with vermillion, and articles of clothing, knives &c., we were able to purchase of them.

The Camanches now began to arrive.

July 22d.—At the Toyash village Colonel Dodge and several of his officers met, agreeably to previous notice, the Toyash chiefs and warriors in council. Council being in order, Colonel Dodge proceeded to speak as follows: "We are the first American officers who have ever come to see the Pawnees; we meet you as friends, not as enemies, to make peace with you, to shake hands with you. The great American captain is at peace with all the white men in the world; he wishes to be at peace with all the red men in the world; we have been sent here to view this country, and to invite you to go to Washington, where the great American chief lives, and make a treaty with him, that you may learn how he wishes to send among you traders, who will bring you guns and blankets, and every thing that you want. The great American chief wishes also to make peace between you and the Osages; you have been at war with the Osages; and to secure peace between you and the Cherokees, Senecas, Delawares, and Chocktaws, and all other red men, that you may all meet together as friends, and not shed each other's blood, as you have done. On our way to your village we met a party of Camanches. We showed to them a white flag, which said to them, "we wish to be friends." Their principal men were gone to hunt; we treated their old men, women, and children, with kindness; we gave them presents; they had many horses; we could have taken their horses from them, but did not; we showed to them that we wanted to be at peace with them; they told us that you were their friends; we were glad to hear of it; we have come to your town, and found you as defenceless as the Camanches; we have treated you as we treated them; the American people show their kindness by actions, and not by words alone; we have been told that a white man was taken prisoner by you last summer; that a boy was made prisoner by you last spring; we have come now to require the boy at your hands, for we are told that he is in your town. Give us the white boy, and we will give you the Pawnee girl that we have brought with us; we wish all that has passed to be put behind us; to be forgotten; we wish to shake hands with you, and be friends; you must now give me a positive and direct answer in regard to the white man who was taken last summer, and the boy who was taken last spring." (Remained in camp.)

The chief We-ter-ra-shah-ro replied. "I know nothing of the man who you say was taken last summer; the white boy is here."

Colonel Dodge resumed, "I wish the boy brought to me; I will then give to you the Pawnee girl; this act, together with all the information you can give concerning the man who was taken last summer, will be the best proof that you can give of the sincerity of your disposition to shake hands and be at peace with us. I cannot leave the country until we obtain possession of the boy, and gain information respecting the man who was taken last summer; his name was Abby; he was taken between the Blue river and the Washita, about this time last year."

Chief. "I know nothing of it. I believe they were Camanches who took the man." On receiving some intelligence from one of his friends, the chief continued: "I remember now, the Oways, who live south, did it."

Colonel Dodge. "Do the Oways hunt on the grounds between the Blue and Washita rivers?"

Chief. "They hunt there, and I have heard that they took the man Abby, and when they got their next camp, they killed him."

Colonel Dodge. "How far do the Oways live from here?"

Chief. "They follow the buffalo as the Camanches do; they have a town." Here a pistol was accidentally fired in the council lodge, which caused much confusion. It was soon explained, however, and business proceeded. The white boy who had been sent for, was brought in and present to Colonel Dodge; the boy was entirely naked, about seven years of age; his name is Matthew Wright Martin.

Chief. "I am glad to shake hands with you, with the red men that you have brought with you, the Osages, Delawares, and Cherokees; the principal chief is not here; but you are as gladly received as he would have welcomed you; the chief has gone to the country of the Pawnee O'Mohaws; he believed that you had gone that way; the father of the Toyash girl went with the chief to seek his daughter."

Colonel Dodge. "How did the Camanches obtain the American flag I saw flying in their camp?"

Chief. "The Pawnees from La Platte sent two flags, one for the Wacoahs, and the other to the Camanches."

Colonel Dodge. "Do the Spaniards come here to trade with you?"

Chief. "They do; they left us not long since, and went west."

Colonel Dodge. "The Americans will give you better and cheaper goods than the Spaniards do. Tell me, if you know, where the ranger (Abby) was taken, and how he was killed?"

Chief. "I have inquired, and have learned this day, that the Indians who live near St. Antoine, in Mexico, captured Abby, and that they killed him on Red river."

Colonel Dodge. "What Indians kill our Santa Fe traders?"

Chief. "There is a roving tribe of very bad Indians called Wakinas; they range north of the country of the Arkansas." Colonel Dodge here presented the girl to her friends, whereupon they conducted her from the council.

Expedition to the Pawnee Pict Village

Colonel Dodge. "I am very much pleased at the exchange of prisoners. I hope the friends of the girl will be happy with her; she is a good girl; I wish her well. I will restore the little boy to his mother; her heart will be glad, and she will think better of the Pawnees; a bright sun has shined on us this day; I hope that Great Spirit will let it shine continually upon us. You have some Osage prisoners; the Osages have some Pawnee prisoners; we will exchange and give you your Pawnee friends, and you shall restore the Osages to their friends. How many Osages have you?"

Chief. "There are Osages here; they are men who were raised here, and do not wish to leave us. The Delaware woman and boy that we took died of the small pox. A great many of the Toyash have died of small pox."

Colonel Dodge. "The American President will have a treaty of peace made between you all; then you will meet and exchange prisoners; this will be done when the next grass grows. The Osages who are with the Pawnees, who then wish to return to the Osages, will be able to return; and the Pawnees who are with the Osages can come back to their people."

Chief. "We wish to have it done soon."

Colonel Dodge. "The American President wishes to see some of each nation shake hands before him; he will give presents to those who visit him, and fix a permanent peace between their nations. Peace cannot be made with all the tribes, till a large white paper be written and signed by the President, and the hands of the chiefs. Will your chiefs go with me now to see the American President? I wish also to take with me some Camanche chiefs. The President will be happy to see you, and will make you, as I told you before, presents of handsome guns, coats, &c."

Much demurring among the chiefs.

Colonel Dodge. "This is the proper time to make peace with the red men and the white men; if you do not seize this opportunity, you may not have another. The bright chain of friendship can now be made bright between all the Indians and the white men."

Chief. "We do not like to pass through the timber; it will be hard for our horses to pass through the thick timber country between us and the white men."

Colonel Dodge. "There are roads—a big road is now being made."

Chief. "We have met here as friends, we hope to remain so. The Great Spirit has seen us as we see now the white men, Cherokees, Osages, Delawares, and Senecas, as friends; we hope to remain so."

Colonel Dodge. "I hope so. How came you by the negro who is here with you?"

Chief. "This Camanche brought him; he found him on the Red River; you can take him, and do as you please with him."

The council here closed.

July 23d.—We-ter-ra-shah-ro, and two other principal men, met Col. Dodge at his tent this morning, and held further talk with him. The four leaders of the bands of Indians who were with us, were present at the talk, and participated therein. Colonel Dodge spoke as follows: "Toyash Chiefs! I told you yesterday that I wished to show you the road that leads to the great American captain, and make you acquainted with the Indians that live on the way thither—have you thought of going with me? Our great father wished you to see the red men who live on the way, that you may be the better able to settle all difficulties with them. You shall be well treated; presents shall be made to you, and you shall be sent back in safety. Peace cannot be made unless some of you go; I am not the great captain, he only can make peace with you, and other red men; I wish only a few of you to go with me, I wish you to go willingly, and as friends; had I chosen to force you to go, it would have been easy for me to do so; you see I do not wish to force you." After a good deal of consultation, one of the chiefs (a Wacoah) consented to go. Here the following interesting ceremony took place. The boy whom we recovered yesterday is the son of the late Judge Martin, of Arkansas, who was killed by a party of Indians some weeks since; the son was with his father on a hunting excursion, and being parted from him, (his death however he did not witness, and is now in ignorance of it;) the boy relates that, after being parted from his father, the Indians who had taken him, were disposed, save one, to kill him; this one shielded him, and took care of him in sickness; Colonel Dodge, as a reward for this noble kindness, gave him a rifle, and at the same time caused the little boy to present him, with his own hand, a pistol.

Expedition to the Pawnee Pict Village

Colonel Dodge now assured the chiefs that they should receive further presents if they would go with him to his country; that he regretted he had nothing of value with him, but begged them to accept some rifles and pistols, which they did, with much evident satisfaction. We-ter-ra-shah-ro, and the other chief men with him here consulted some time together on the subject of visiting the President. We-ter-ra-shah-ro spoke. "We have been at war with the nations which we see around us to-day: we wish now to make peace with them."

Colonel Dodge answered him. "It is the wish of the President that you make peace with them; that you present to each other clean hands; it is to effect this that I wish you to go with me."

The chief resumed. "We wish much to make peace with the Osages, we have been long at war with them; we wish to see the lands of the Creeks and Cherokees also, to shake hands with all. We want now to hear those Indians who came with you speak to us." The chief men of the four parties now spoke as follows:

Dutch, the Cherokee. "I am now going to tell you what the chief of the Cherokees bade me say to you if we met as friends. He says to you, his people wish to come to you without fear, and that you should visit them without fear. My heart is glad that we are all willing to be friends; a long time ago it was so, there was no war between us. I am rejoiced, and my people will be rejoiced, when they hear that it may be so again. Look at me, you see I speak the truth, I have nothing more to say."

Beatte, leader of the Osage band. "We came for peace—I have brought a few Osages, who were not afraid to come among you, with hearts inclined for peace. We look on our friend (Colonel Dodge) as our father; he is a true father to us all. I hope you will believe all that he says to you, and trust that he will prove a father to you. We wish you to visit our people, to see how we live since the white men have been our friends; they have made us happy, they will make you happy: you should go with our father as he wishes; you must then come and see the Osages. I have said all that I can say."

Monpisha, an Osage youth, spoke to the Toyash men. "We shake hands with pleasure. I am nothing but a boy, my father was an Osage chief: we wish to be your brothers—dogs fight—we wish to be peaceable men, and friends. Our good father has made, in coming to you, a great road; we hope it will never be stained with blood. My father told me he was once a wild Indian; that white men taught him to be happy, instructed him how to build houses, raise cattle, and live like white men. I was sent to the white man's school, (missionary school,) was taught to read and write: this will be extended to you, if you make peace with white men; your buffalo will be gone in a few years; your great father the President will give you cattle, and teach you how to live without buffalo."

George Bullett (Pon-da-gne-se) spoke. "When I tell the Delawares that we are friends, and can now hunt without warring together, they will be happy our children will hereafter be happy, and not fear each other; we will no more fear the prairie Indian, and you will not be afraid of us."

Colonel Dodge resumed. "I am glad to hear what our friends say to you. I must say to you now that I am very sorry that a few of our horses got into your cornfield last night; I shall pay you for the damage done—it is not my wish to disturb your property in any manner. White men will always be just to you. I must also repeat that I regretted that the pistol was accidently fired in the council lodge yesterday: I did not wish to alarm your people; I was pleased with the coolness of your chief; he was not alarmed. I wish you now to consider if some of you will go with me."

The chiefs signified that they would go home and decide who should accompany the command on its march back, and accordingly left our camp.

Many Camanches arrived to-day; amongst them the principal chief Ta-we-que-nah, and two other chiefs. Colonel Dodge held the following talk with them in his tent:

"The great American captain has sent me to view this country, and to offer the hand of friendship to all the red men who are here; he wishes to see you all at peace with each other; he desires you to come and see him, that he may fix a permanent peace with your tribes; he will make you presents, and he will send traders among you who will serve you with a great many things that you want to make you happy. The President, who is a good father to you, wishes to see you at peace with the Osages, Cherokees, Delawares, and all red men. We have endeavored to give you evidence of our friendship—we did so when we passed your camp; you were not at home, your women and children were defenceless; we treated them kindly, we confided in you too. Our sick men we left behind near your camp."

Ta-we-que-nah replied. "I passed a night in your camp with your sick men; they treated us with kindness."

Colonel Dodge. "You say that the Indians over Red river are your enemies, they kill you when you meet; these are Mexican Indians, and do not make treaties with our great father the President; but he will protect you when you make peace with the Osages and other tribes that have been at war against you. The flag that you have, came to you from the great father at Washington. The Pawnee O'Mohaws have such a flag, and all other red men who are our friends; whenever you show it, you will be known as friends. I was glad to see the flag over your camp."

The chief spoke. "I wish to be at peace with you; there are many bands of Camanches, I shall visit them all this year, and will say to them what you have said to me; they will all be glad to make peace with you; I am an old man now, but never since I was a boy did I kill one of your people. You ask me who killed the ranger, Abby; I can tell you, for I remember when this white man was taken; the Texas Camanches took this white men, and carried him over the Red river, and there killed him."

Colonel Dodge. "I wish some of you to go with me, that you may see our country, and that peace may be made strongly between you and the red men, as well as between ourselves; the Pawnee O'Mohaws met the Osages, and Delawares, and Cherokees, on our lands, and there made peace; they were enemies before, they are now friends, and do not hate each other. We wish you to come to us, and make, in the same way, peace with us."

Ta-we-que-nah. You have a girl who was taken from our friends, the Kiowas. I have a Spanish girl; I will give you the Spanish girl, in exchange for the Kiowa girl that you have brought with you."

Colonel Dodge. "I wish to secure your friendship, and the friendship of the Kiowas. I wish you to accompany me. I wish some of the Kiowas to go also; but I do not mean to sell the girl to them; I mean to give her to her relations and friends without price; I will give the girl to her tribe; they shall see how much their friends we are."

Ta-we-que-nah. "If I go with you, I shall be afraid to come back through the timber."

Colonel Dodge. "I pledge myself that you shall be safely conducted back."

Ta-we-que-nah. "I cannot go myself; my brother will go with you."

Here the talk was interrupted by a band of some twenty or thirty Kiowas rushing on horseback into camp, and almost into the door of Colonel Dodge's tent; the squaws and children fled in great alarm. The indignation of these Indians against the Osages had kindled to a great pitch, and could scarcely be kept in respectful bounds in their relation to us. The Osages, not many months previously, had murdered a large number of the women and children of the Kiowas whilst the men were absent hunting. We held in possession, of which they were informed, a Kiowa girl, who was taken on the occasion of the massacre alluded to: the Kiowas having just arrived, were not aware of the intention on our part to restore the girl, and consequently presented themselves in a warlike shape, they caused many a man in camp to stand by his arms. Colonel Dodge, however, immediately addressed them with assurances of our friendly disposition, and gradually led them into gentleness. They are a bold, warlike-looking Indian. Some of their horses are very fine; they ride well, and were admirably equipped to-day for fight or flight; their bows strung, and quivers filled with arrows. They kept their saddles chiefly. A relation of the Kiowa girl embraced her, and shed tears of joy at the intimation that she should be restored to her father and friends, She proves to be a relation of one of the chiefs. An arrangement was now made for a general council, to be held the next day, between the Camanche, Toyash, and Kiowa nations. (Remained in camp.)

July 24th.—At 10 o'clock the chiefs of the council began to assemble at the place appointed for the meeting, which was in a wood about two hundred yards from our camp. The father of the Kiowa girl having learned that she was to be restored, in a speech addressed to the Kiowas, whose numbers every moment increased, gave vent to his joy, and praise of his white friends. All came mounted and armed. Many of our officers were present. There were not less than two thousand mounted and armed Indians around the council. Great excitement prevailed among the Indians, but especially with the Kiowas, who embraced Colonel Dodge, and shed tears of gratitude for the restoration of their relative. An uncle of Wa-ha-sep-ah, a man of about forty years of age, was touchingly eager in his demonstrations, frequently throwing his arms around Colonel Dodge, and weeping over his shoulders; then invoking blessings upon him, in a manner the most graceful and ardent: the women came in succession, and embraced the girl, who was seated among the chiefs. The council being now in order, and the pipes having made their rounds, Colonel Dodge addressed the Camanche chief, who sat on his right, and who interpreted his words to the Kiowas, whilst a Toyash Indian, who speaks the Caddo tongue, communicated with the Toyash men from Chiom, one of our Cherokee friends, who speaks English and Caddo: "I am glad to see together the great chief of the Camanche nation, the chiefs of the Kiowa and Toyash people, and the American officers who are with me; we have been strangers until now. I am glad to meet the captain of the Camanches, (Ta-we-que-nah.) You must be a great man, and have much power with all the tribes around you. I ask you to urge to these Indians what I have said to you, that we are your friends, and that, to secure our mutual and lasting friendship, it is better for some of each of you to go with me, as I have before mentioned to you."

Here another band of Kiowas, about sixty in number, rode up, led by a principal man, handsomely dressed. He wore a Spanish red cloth mantle, prodigious feathers, and leggings that followed his heels like an ancient train. Another of the chiefs of the new band was very showily arrayed; he wore a perfectly white dressed deer skin hunting shirt, trimmed profusely with fringe of the same material, and beautifully bound with blue beads, over which was thrown a cloth mantle of blue and crimson, with leggings and moccasins entirely of beads. Our new friends shook hands all round, and seated themselves with a dignity and grace that would well become senators of a more civilized conclave.

T. B. Wheelock

Colonel Dodge resumed. "Kiowa chiefs! I herewith present to you your relation; receive her as the best evidence of the sincere friendship of Americans. Our great captain, the President, purchased this girl of the Osages, who took her from your people, and has sent me to restore her to the arms of her friends who love her. The Camanche chief, Ta-we-que-nah, offered me, yesterday, in exchange for her, a Spanish girl; I would not accept of his offer, for the delivery of the girl is an act of justice, and is but one of the many acts of kindness that the great American captain will be glad to show to you. You, and the Indians who came with us, have long been at war with each other; it is time you were at peace together; it is the wish of the President to secure a permanent good understanding among you all. He will send traders among you. You want guns, blankets, &c., the buffalo are becoming scarce; there are less and less every year. You shall have cattle which you can keep with you; you can plant your corn and cultivate the soil, as the Cherokees and other Indians do. Here is a young man (Mr. Chadwick) who has come out with me to see you, and who will return next summer, and bring goods and trade with you. I now wish you to consider the invitation given you to go with me, and assure you you shall receive presents, and be safely conducted through the timber country." One of the chiefs inquired, "Will you go to-morrow?"

Colonel Dodge. "I wish to go as soon as practicable, as we have far to go; I wish you to visit General Leavenworth, another of your friends, and a captain under the great captain; he wishes to see you; he has never seen you; I should be glad to introduce to him two chiefs from each nation, or one chief and some of the warriors of each people."

Titche-totche-cha, chief of the Kiowas, signified his willingness to go. We-ter-rah-shah-ro, an old chief, (70 years of age,) urged his red brethren to rely on the truth of Colonel Dodge's words: "he is a good man," said he; "believe his words."

The father of the Kiowa girl begged Colonel Dodge to accept of a present, which the Colonel declined, repeating what he had before said, that he did not wish for ransom or reward; that the child was given to the father as an evidence of the good feeling of his people for them.

Expedition to the Pawnee Pict Village

Titche-totche-cha spoke. "The American captain has spoken well to-day; the white men have shown themselves our friends. If a white man ever comes to my country, he shall be kindly treated; if he wants a horse, or any thing that I have, he shall not pay for it; I will give him what he wants. The council here closed, we returned to our camp, and left the Indians to decide in regard to accompanying us. It is on all accounts desirable to move from here: our provisions prove unhealthy for our men, consisting entirely of green corn, and dried horse and buffalo meat: the weather has been excessively hot and dry; our men, many of them sick, are without a physician or medicines; two or three officers are and have been for several days ill of fevers, The Camanche squaws are very troublesome, they steal every thing that they can secrete. The Toyash women are infinitely more respectable; the difference in these three tribes seems to be somewhat thus: the Camanche is an arrogant, jealous, savage Don; the Toyash, a savage farmer; whilst the Kiowa, more chivalrie, impulsive and daring, than either, reminds one of the bold clannish Highlander, whose very crimes are made, by the poet, captivating; this tribe has roamed more towards the Rocky mountains until within a few years past.

July 25th.—The chiefs of the three tribes early visited our camp. Colonel Dodge presented them with guns and pistols. Fifteen Kiowas including the chief Titche-totche-cha, were the first mounted and equipped, ready to march with us; the Camanche chief very cautious, and apparently suspicious, deferred till late, when four Camanches, a squaw, and our early acquaintance, the Spaniard, joined us; there was much delay on the part of the Toyash. At length the old chief We-ter-ra-shah-ro, a Wacoah chief, (of a small band, who speak the same language as the Toyash people, and live near their town,) and two Toyash warriors, rode into our camp prepared to move with us.

The command, with the Indians, the white boy, and the negro in company, marched at 3 o'clock, halted at 5 o'clock, and encamped on a creek six miles east.

July 26th.—Marched at half past 7 o'clock: our guide, the Pawnee O'Mohaw, who had promised to remain with us, left us; he was no loss, for he had led us over a uselessly long route, over rocks, and hills, through deep ravines, all of which our guide to-day, a Toyash has avoided, and, in place thereof, we have passed through a beautiful valley four or five miles in width, over an open, level prairie, leaving the granite roads on our right and left in the mountains; course to-day east, distance twenty-one miles; water scarce, grass very much destroyed by heat and dry weather; encamped on a stream of good water, good grazing; severe shower of rain, the first that has blessed us for many days; parched corn and dried buffalo meat our fare; health of command tolerably good. From conversation to-day with one of the Indians, (Ski-sa-ro-ka, an intelligent Toyash,) we learn that their nation lived formerly south, that their oldest men were born there, and that they and the Camanches have long been in habits of friendly intercourse; the Camanches exchange buffalo meat for the agricultural productions of the Toyash; the Camanches not much liked by the Toyash; they cheat them, and ride away. The Kiowas, a newer acquaintance, more honest and gentle. The Camanches of Texas a much more powerful tribe than those on this side of the Red river; they are called the Ho-ishe Camanche.

July 27th. — Marched at half past 7 o'clock, course east, distance twenty-three miles; reached the sick camp at 4 o'clock, found Lieuts. Izard and Moore both sick with fevers; also Mr. Catlin very ill: twenty-nine sick men in both camps. Lieut. Wheelock's servant, left sick on the 19th inst., died in our absence. Our road to-day lay through a valley; occasional interruptions from timbered creeks and small thickets, until we reached "Roaring river," a short stream, but containing a considerable volume of water; empties into the Red river. The Camanches who set out with us, left us to-day, on account, as they say, of the sickness of the squaw. The Spaniard, who seems to belong to that tribe more than with any other, remains with us. These Indians seem well contented, and move without restraint, encamping with us at night, and setting out with the command, or after it has marched, as they please. Col. Dodge and all the officers unable to account for not hearing from Gen. Leavenworth. From the Short supplies taken, we have reason to expect to hear from or meet with our wagons — our buffalo meat very short, and no game as yet.

July 28th. — Broke up the sick camp, and marched at half past 9 o'clock, with the whole command, taking again with us the Senecas, who had been left to hunt for the men left at this camp. Excessive hot weather; 43 sick, 7 in litters; course east by north, distance 12 miles. The heat to-day has been overpowering, both to men and horses; water tolerable; course north, from our trace going out; camp to-night about six miles from former trace.

Col. Dodge sent an express in search of Gen. Leavenworth, to inform him of our return from the Pawnee villages. Col. Dodge resolves to wait in the buffalo range for orders from Gen. Leavenworth. Deer abundant to-day; one or two killed. One of the men killed a panther yesterday; passed to-day many hills of gypsum.

July 29th. — Marched to-day at 8 o'clock, east by north, distance fifteen miles; provisions very short. At 12 o'clock the cry of buffalo was heard, and never was the cheering sound of land better welcomed by wearied mariners, than this by our hungry columns. The command was halted, and some went together; the report of Beatte's rifle, and the fall of a fat cow; halted at 4 o'clock; killed two more buffaloes. Passed to-day more plaster of Paris; road to-day over open, rolling prairies, between two forks of the Washita; met a small party of Toyash Indians. Our red friends suffer exceedingly from the heat of the sun; we covered them this morning with shirts.

July 30th. — Marched at 8 o'clock; weather excessively hot; course northeast, fourteen miles; course interrupted by frequent deep gullies totally impassable for wagons. Nine miles from camp passed the Washita; good water to-day; encamped on a fine stream; large fishes visible from the bank; timbered creeks, black jack, elm, and mulberry trees; more gypsum.

July 31st. — Marched at half past eight o'clock; men in fine spirits; abundance of buffalo meat; course northeast; distance 10 miles; encamped on a branch of the Canadian; three buffaloes killed this morning; no news yet from express; anxiously looked for; face of country rolling prairie; frequent deep gullies; one of the Kiowas killed three buffaloes with three arrows.

August 1st. — The signal for advance was sounded at half past eight o'clock; course north by east; distance 15 miles; halted at half past one o'clock; 10 miles from camp crossed the Canadian; plenty of water to-day; passed the Canadian about 100 miles from our ford going out; abundance of buffalo, immense herds in every direction from the camp; men employed at night in drying meat; officers and men fortunate who have been provident enough to save a small quantity of corn for parching. Camp alarmed this evening by the cry of "secure your horses from the buffalo;" a herd was rushing upon our camp, around which our horses had just been picketed, and had approached within two hundred yards of us, when our mounted sentinels changed their direction, and thus saved us from another "stampede." We have been fortunate in having had but one occurrence of this not uncommon evil with bodies of horse on the prairies.

August 2d. — Rest! Welcome rest for men and horses; occupied in killing and drying buffalo meat for the anticipated march to Fort Leavenworth; probable distance thither 400 miles; our men not unfrequently lost in hunting; in several instances absent from camp all night; our men find an excellent substitute for tea and coffee in a wild sage plant; we still have the advantage of being not at all troubled with flies or musquitos; the nights are so cool that the covering of a blanket is pleasant.

August 3d. — Moved a mile at half past ten o'clock, for change of grazing, and police; our horses are in bad order, so much so that it is feared they may not be equal to a march to Fort Leavenworth; may possibly be compelled to move to Fort Gibson to recruit and shoe them. Little Martin flourishes, and is a great favorite in the command; he is an uncommonly fine boy.

August 4th. — The command marched at half past eight o'clock, southerly direction, eight miles along the Canadian, in search of buffalo; they have fled from the vicinity of our last camp; passed large herds of buffalo; the Kiowas dashed in amongst them, and killed, with their arrows, a vast many of them; grass very much dried, scarce affording subsistence for our horses; Colonel Dodge has decided on marching to Fort Gibson. The prairie took fire to-day near our camp, and was with difficulty extinguished.

August 5th. — Rested for the day; men employed in curing meat the express to Gen. Leavenworth returned. Intelligence from Captain

Expedition to the Pawnee Pict Village

Dean of 3d infantry, announces the death of Gen. Leavenworth; he died at his camp near "Cross Timbers," on the 21st of July; Lieut. McClure, of this regiment, died at the Washita on the 20th of July; bilious fevers; one hundred and fifty men sick at the Washita.

August 6th. — Marched at 8 o'clock for the fort at the mouth of Little river; course southeast, distance twenty-three miles; road through "Cross Timbers." This is a timbered thicket, small black jack saplings so close as to frequently require the axe to make a road for a horseman. Five litters in our train; men in them extremely ill. Col. Dodge sent an express to Col. Kearney, who is at Camp Smith, near the mouth of the Washita, directing him to move his command to Fort Gibson, herds of buffalo broke and rebroke through our columns to-day; encamped in timber, in the bottom of a branch of Little river; found excellent grazing in the pea vines; litters came up several hours after the command.

August 7th. — Our columns started at 8 o'clock; course south by east; gained eighteen miles; still in the "Cross Timbers," which promise to continue till we strike the road to Fort Gibson; a few small prairies interspersed amongst the severest black jack thickets. Our route to-day has been on the dividing ridge between the Canadian and Little rivers. Scarcity of water; fortunately found at 4 o'clock good water and grazing.

August 8th. — Marched at 8 o'clock, halted at 3 o'clock; distance eighteen miles; course east by south; exceedingly warm day; stubborn thickets; crossed and encamped in the bottom of Little river; shallow stream, narrow bed, miry shores, no water from morning till the halt for the night; passed many creeks, the beds of which were entirely dry; our horses looked up and down their parched surfaces, and the men gazed in vain at the willows ahead, which proved to mark only where water had been. The timber is larger here; black walnut and sycamore; lime and freestone; the woods abound to-day in plums, and a variety of finely flavored grapes; no longer any trace of the buffalo; sick report, numbers, thirty men and three officers.

August 9th. — Marched at the usual hour, and made twenty miles in a northeast course; Cross Timbers, but more open than for the last three days; tolerable supply of water; soil sandy; encamped at 4 o'clock in open timber, near where we struck the road from Fort Gibson to the Washita, which was 3 miles from the post at the mouth of Little River.

August 10th.—Dragoon camp "Canadian." We drew from Lt. Holmes, commander of the infantry camp "Canadian," at the mouth of Little river, provisions for four days; Lt. Holmes well advanced with his buildings; one block-house, and quarters for one company, erected; vast many sick; on our sick list thirty. (Remained in camp.)

August 11th.—Marched at 8 o'clock; left our sick, whom we brought in litters, at the infantry camp; gained on the road to Fort Gibson 22 miles; our men happy, with pork and flour.

August 12th.—Command moved at 8 o'clock; express returned from Camp Smith; Lt. Col. Kearney reports many sick; 71 for duty, 41 sick; 8 for duty at Camp Washita, and 70 sick; many of our horses disabled; led by men in rear of the columns; tolerable water; wholly in pools. It is worthy of remark, that the mules of the command look better than when we started on the campaign, while it would be difficult to select ten horses in good order. The command ordered to walk and ride one hour alternately; this relieves the horses.

August 13th.—Marched at ½ past 7 o'clock and reached the Creek settlements at the north fork of the Canadian, 17 miles. The Toyash and Kiowas met the Creeks this evening, and shook hands with them; we purchased, here, corn for our horses; informed here, by a citizen, that the mother of Little Martin has recently offered two thousand dollars for his recovery; she will soon be made happy by his restoration, without ransom or reward.

August 14th.—We marched, at 8 o'clock, 20 miles to our former camp, ("Rendezvous,") from whence the regiment started on the 21st June. Our horses are exceedingly worn, though somewhat aided to-day by the corn we gave them yesterday at the North fork. The season in unfortunately late for grazing; it is only in timber that tolerable grass is found; extraordinary heat to-day; the breeze comes against the face and hands with an unpleasant heat, so that one turns from it as from the keen blasts of winter; water scarce and in pools; our men present a sorry figure, but one that looks like service; many of them literally half naked; sick list reduced to nineteen.

Expedition to the Pawnee Pict Village

August 15th.—Marched at ½ past 7 o'clock; an officer was sent in advance to purchase corn; the command marched 14 miles, and encamped three miles from the west bank of the Arkansas. Col. Dodge and staff, together with the Indians, crossed the river late in the evening, and reached Fort Gibson.

August 16th.—Fort Gibson; Major Mason and three companies ordered this side of the river; Capt. Sumner and three companies directed to remain in camp on the west side of the Arkansas.

August 24th.—Col. Kearney's command arrived yesterday; great number of sick men, and worn down horses; officers belonging to it are Capt. Trenor, Lieut. Swords, (sick,) Lieut. Van Deveer, (sick,) Lieut. Eastman, (sick,) Lieuts. Bowman, Ury, and Kingsbury; Assistant Surgeon Hailes, (very sick.)

Runners have been sent to the chiefs of the Osages, Cherokees, Creeks, Choctaws, &c., for the purpose of assembling them in council with the Indians who have accompanied us. Our friends from the prairie are in good health, and are apparently contented. Little Martin is still with Col. Dodge; and the negro we brought from the Toyash village has been delivered to his master.

T.B. WHEELOCK,
1st Lieut. Dragoons.